Leaving
Islam

Printed: 112 pages, 6" x 9", perfect binding, cream interior paper (60# weight), black and white interior ink, white exterior paper (100# weight), full-color exterior ink

Publisher: Lulu.com

Rights Owner: Emjays Graphics

Copyright: © 2007 Standard Copyright License

Language: English

Country: United States

Story of Khalil

Truth is Jesus; Jesus is truth; Lord is Jesus; Jesus is Lord.

Before I tell you how and why I became a Christian, I would like to tell you about the kind of Muslim family in which I was raised.

MY CHILDHOOD

My name is David now, but I was born under a different name—Khalil—in a Pakistani family. We were a Muslim family of nine. I have four older sisters and two younger brothers. I used to pray, fast, give charity/zakat, but these religious activities did not give me the peace I was searching for in my life.

My mother taught me Arabic as a second language at the age of five; Urdu was my first language. By the age of six I had read the entire Quran and also memorized some of its chapters. I constantly recited the Quran as I grew older, and read some particular surahs that my father told me to read on a regular basis to fulfill my wishes and solve my problems.

I read all this without knowing what it really meant. Most Muslims will tell you that it is good to do this purely on the basis that reading it in Arabic will please god, which I find illogical and with no basis whatsoever.

MY RELIGIOUS FAMILY

My older sisters were really into religion like my parents and they always wanted me and my younger brothers to do the same. I listened to them and did what I was told. Despite all the religious acts, I was not very happy inside my heart about what I was doing. I always thought about the fact that there are hundreds of different religions around the world; how can be Islam the best, true and direct way to god? Nevertheless, I continued reading the Quran, fasting and praying.

When I was twelve, my oldest sister was forced to get married to a Muslim man who was the son of my father's best friend. Although my sister loved a high school friend who essentially loved her as well, she had no choice but to marry this man. The problem was that this high school friend was not a Muslim.

At that time I was not very happy with the decision my parents made, but I was too young to do any thing at that time. My sister Sumaiya was very sad to loose her sweetheart, but she could not do any thing either. After a couple of years, I came to know that the person my sister loved was a Christian. I also was able to talk to him and realized that he was a great person with sincerity and purity of heart.

As I grew older I started loving my religion with all my heart because I was accustomed to believing in Islam, praying, fasting and celebrating the typical festive holidays of Islam with my family without realizing that it was not the true religion and is essentially in vain.

MY CAREER

After I finished my twelfth year of schooling, I started studying medicine at Agha Khan University in Karachi, Pakistan. My dream was to go to one of the best universities in the United States and complete my degree. I had aspirations to do wonderful things for my country after I returned.

Unfortunately, my parents were not very happy with what I desired. However, when I received admission from my first choice of medical university, I made up my mind that I would convince my parents and go to the US. As one of my aunts (my father's sister) lives in the US, I talked my parents into moving to United States for few years and would go back.

ARRIVAL IN THE UNITED STATES

I finally came to the US at the age of nineteen and started school. I had to live a very typical life spending time getting my education and holding onto a part time job so that I could afford to put myself through school. Fortunately, I did not have to worry about rent and food because I was living with my aunt. But that did not last very long. My aunt and her family had to move to a different state for some reason so I had to get a place of my own. I could not afford to rent a place by myself, but God in his mercy and grace provided me with a place to live. One of my classmates, Roy, was looking for a roommate. I asked him if I could live with him and he agreed. I did not know him very well until I moved and started living with him. He is one of the greatest people I have ever met.

A GREAT FRIEND

Soon we become very good friends. We lived together, studied together and had a lot of similarities. The only difference we had was our "religion." He was a Christian and I was a Muslim. Because of this religious difference, my heart wanted to avoid him as (according to our religious leaders) he was a polytheist and worshiper of three gods, among whom was Jesus "son of god." Nevertheless, I continued to be good to him as I always had the golden rule in my heart: "Treat others as you want yourself to be treated."

What always impressed me the most about Roy was that he always talked about loving others, helping the needy and being ready to suffer.

CHALLENGES BEGUN!

He used to read the Bible every evening and it surprised me every time I saw him with it. As a Muslim I read the Quran almost every day and prayed regularly, but seeing a Christian seriously reading the Bible and praying was a shock to my eyes. One day I got really curious about how much he really knew about his religion and the Bible.

DIFFERENCES BETWEEN ISLAM AND CHRISTIANITY

JESUS DIED ON THE CROSS!

I decided to challenge Roy about his belief as a Christian that Jesus died on the cross. According to the Quran, Christ did not die on the cross.

The teachings of the Quran in this regard may be summed up as follows:

1- Christ was neither crucified nor killed by the Jews, not withstanding certain apparent circumstances that produce illusions in the minds of some of the enemies.

2- Jesus was taken up to god, which means god raised him up. (Quran 4:157, 158 and 3:55 and 4:157).

Christians also believe that Jesus was resurrected three days after being crucified on the cross (Good Friday and Easter Sundays are the days when Christians remember and celebrate this). I was very sure that I could make Roy's belief completely invalid. But after investigating the facts surrounding the death of Christ, I was really amazed by how clear it is that Jesus Christ did die on the cross.

"Blessed be the god and father of our lord Jesus Christ who according to his abundant mercy has begotten us again to a living hope through the resurrection of the Jesus Christ from the dead..." (Peter 1:3 NKJV).

Based on the historical evidence and knowledge about how Jesus was crucified, there can be no way to deny the death of the Christ.

TRINITY

After this discovery, I had a question in my mind whether the Quran or the Bible is right. Of course I was still picking the Quran because this presentation in itself cannot change my belief.

A few weeks later, I decided to fight with Roy on different tasks about our beliefs. Christians believe in trinity (Father, son, Holy Spirit). As a member of the trinity, Jesus is viewed as god himself whereas Muslims do not believe in the trinity and Jesus as a god.

Jesus was a prophet and servant of God, like Prophet Mohammed, who also was a prophet of God and guided mankind.

This time our discussion was much longer than the first. Nowhere, ever, did Jesus Christ claim he is the literal son of god (part of trinity). But Roy said that it is the truth that Jesus is the son of god. In the Old Testament Isaiah prophesized that a child would be born who would be called "*mighty god*" (Isaiah 9:6), but this is not the only testament supporting the duty of Christ. The most common title for Jesus was "son of man."

According to the New Testament, Jesus was worshipped shortly after his birth (Matthew 2:11) during his ministry (Mathew 14:33; john 9:38), and after his resurrection from the dead (Mathew 28:9, 28:17), yet he never told his worshippers to stop what they were doing. When he was asked whether he was the son of god, he answered,

"I am and you will see the son of men sitting at the right of the mighty one and coming on the clouds of heaven" (Mark 14:62).

```
   The          Is Not
  Father  ———————————————  The Son
       \        Is     Is      /
        \                     /
     Is Not      God       Is Not
          \       Is       /
           \              /
            The Holy
             Spirit
```

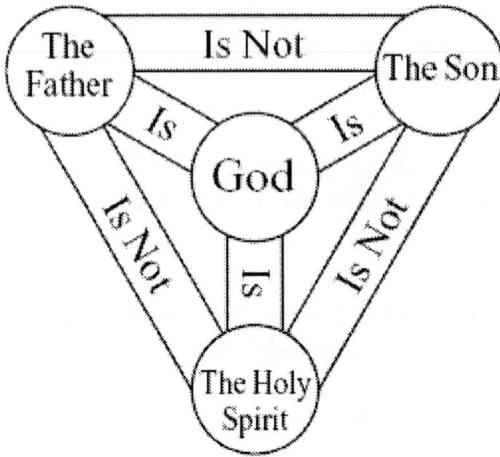

The trinity says that god is both father and son. This
does not make him two gods; these are two separate
ways in which God experiences love, two roles or
two "modes of being." Because the Bible speaks
equally about the Holy Spirit as God's way of being
present with us, the Holy Spirit is included in the
trinity, representing the presence of the father with
the son and with us. God's presence is always
personal, so it is best expressed as a person in the
trinity, rather than simply as something impersonal
like "Gods power."

*"And Jesus, when he was baptized, went up
straight way out of the water: and the heavens were
open unto him, and he saw the spirit of god
descending a like dove, and lighting upon him and a
voice from heaven, saying, this is my beloved son, in
whom I am well pleased."*

I also found out from historical evidence
that the distinction is often described as a difference
in "origin." This means that the father is the source

of the trinity. This single source is the basis of god's unity. The son is begotten from him and the spirit proceeds from him.

After actually reading parts of the new testament itself instead of merely reading Muslim books on the topic, I came to agree with Roy's claim: both the new testament in general and Christ himself claimed that Jesus is god.

BIBLE IS RIGHT AND IS THE TRUE BOOK OF GOD

As a Muslim I knew that the Quran was the uncorrupted word of God transmitted from God (Allah) himself through the prophet of Islam, whereas the Bible is corrupted and no sensible person could ever trust the Bible. Roy said that the Bible is 100 percent the faultless word of god, whereas I said that the Bible is textually corrupted and subject to distorted interpretation.

Roy offered me some responses to my argument.

There are many variations of the Bible obtained from more than five thousand Greek manuscripts. Further, there is a large amount of early manuscript evidence and such occurrences of evidence between those manuscripts can reconstruct the Bible and be certain about ninety five percent of the original content. Also, the quotations and the references of the New Testament are so many that we can reconstruct practically all of it from early quotations alone. Roy also said that there are whole copies of the books available from around three centuries after Christ's death and the accuracy is actually closer to ninety nine percent. He also claimed that there are a lot of fragments of manuscripts that can be dated within a couple of centuries after Christ's death, which we have in our possession even now.

His great convincing argument blew me away and I thought he did it all and won. I investigated that the new testaments are not at all different from the original manuscripts. But I did not want to give up. I decided to challenge him on some more issues that I definitely thought were the truth, but unfortunately they were not.

DOES JESUS PAY FOR THE SINS OF MILLLIONS OF PEOPLE WHO BELIEVE IN HIM?

Christ redeemed us from the curse of the law by becoming by becoming a curse for us, for it is written: "cursed is everyone who is hung on a tree." (Galatians 3:13)

As time passed by, my mind and heart both became confused about what is the truth and vice versa. As a Muslim I also believed that all of mankind is born pure and he or she is responsible for his or her own sins and not someone else's. In the Quran it clearly says that all the controversies about dogma and faith will disappear when we appear before god; he will judge not by what we profess, but by what we are.

How could it be possible that someone else would be able to pay for my sins? And not only mine, but the sins of the entire world? I told Roy that each person is responsible for his or her own actions and that no one else can atone for them. However, you can pray to god for his mercy and forgiveness on behalf of another person. The prophet Mohammed and some others (the innocent babies who have passed away) are given the special privilege to intercede on behalf of their parents on the Day of Judgment. This is in accord with the throne verse in the Quran. Thus, with God's graceful permission, they may have a specially bestowed privilege of pleading on behalf of others and begging for God's forgiveness for them on the Day of Judgment. This is known as intercession (shaf'at).

Causing an innocent man to suffer for the rest of the world's bad deeds, crimes, and wrong ways of living is not right! Here started Roy's arguments and claims.

In him we have redemption through his blood, the forgiveness of sins, according to the riches of his grace which he made to abound towards us it all wisdom and prudence… (Ephesians1:7, 8).

It was just impossible to believe that God, the creator of this Universe, would allow one of his most beloved messengers to die in order to pay for the sins of all the people in the world. But the discussion and arguments offered by Roy forced my mind to believe that Jesus is the only one who pays for the sins of the people who believe in him.

For God so loved the world that he gave his one and only Son, that whoever believes in him shall not perish but have eternal life.
(John 3:16)

For it is by grace you have been saved, through faith and this not from yourselves, it is the gift of God--
(Ephesians 2:8, 9)

OTHER DIFFERENCES

Other than these four major differences, there were a lot of other differences in our beliefs. Muslims believe that God has informed only ninety-nine of his beautiful names (attributes). Many of them depict his beautiful aspects (Jamal), some of them depict his power, authority and grandeur (Jalal), whereas Christians emphasize the beautiful aspects of God (God is love). In Islam, pilgrimage is one of the five pillars and is obligatory, whereas in Christianity pilgrimage is not obligatory.

STRUGGLE AND PRAYERS FOR THE GUIDENCE TOWARDS THE TRUE PATH

Our discussion lasted a few more weeks. In the meantime, I persisted in asking God to guide me. I began to see that it was possible for Jesus to be the God. Intellectually, I accepted all the claims of the Christian faith, but in my heart I still feared being struck dead for calling the Almighty God "My Father." From the depth of my heart, I prayed to God to show me the right path and the truth.

I started waking up in the mornings with tears because of the dreams I was having. Thinking that the religion I believed in for so many years of my life is not true made me felt very guilty. Now I needed a powerful god to help me with my battle. I was hoping that God would come and fight for me, showing Islam to be the correct path, but unfortunately it didn't happen.

I asked again and again for any sign that would show me whether **Jesus** or **Allah** is true. Suddenly, one morning I started to see lots of crosses everywhere, on my mirror, on my plate, on my clothes and hands. These crosses were coming and going. I was really shocked. I didn't know if my eyes were playing tricks on me or it was really the truth.

"Because he loves me," says the LORD, "I will rescue him; I will protect him, for he acknowledges my name."

I prayed to God that if the next day I see the same crosses again then I will believe that Jesus is our lord and God and I will become a Christian. That day was a very hard day for me. I couldn't sleep at night. Finally, when I went to bed at 2 AM, God came in my dream and said that he really liked what I was doing and he is with me. Then I saw a picture of a man on the cross; he was all blooded and his open arms called and welcomed me. That was it. The next morning when I woke up it was amazing that I saw the same crosses in the same places again. That was the end of my life as a Muslim.

JESUS IS MY LORD!

Jesus replied, "If anyone loves me, he will obey my teaching. My Father will love him, and we will come to him and make our home with him" (John 14:23).

That was the start of a journey, of getting to know my lord Jesus better, accepting him as my savior and his full payment for my sins. I am grateful to God for providing this friend Roy, who disciplined me, and taught me to live a victorious life rich in worship and thanksgiving.

But if anyone obeys his word, God's love is truly made complete in him. This is how we know we are in him:
(John 2:5)

After I accepted Jesus, there was a peace in my heart and I was very happy and satisfied. From the beginning, Christians were in my heart as wonderful people. The man whom my sister loved and Roy were both wonderful people and excellent human beings.

Be devoted to one another in brotherly love. Honor one another above yourselves.

But this was not it. There was more. I had to tell my parents, who love me to death, about what happened in my life over past two years. They were eagerly waiting for me in Pakistan. I decided to spread this message to as many people as I could. There are billions of lives/souls that need to be saved.

"I tell you the truth," Jesus replied, "no one who has left home or brothers or sisters or mother or father or children or fields for me and the gospel will fail to receive a hundred times as much in this present age (homes, brothers, sisters, mothers, children and fields and with them, persecutions) and in the age to come, eternal life."

VISIT TO PAKISTAN

It was during my summer vacation when I decided to go to Pakistan for a month. I told everything to my parents and my siblings. When they heard this they were all in tears. My mom screamed, "What happened? What happened to my son?" Why did we sent him to the US? Everybody yelled at me and was trying to convince me not to make this mistake while I tried to challenge them that this is not a mistake but the truth and the message of God.

21

My family did not accept me at first, but when they realized that I was totally into Christianity and the Lord Jesus being God, over the years they started respecting my belief and I was considered an outcast.

Over the years, the mutual respect has resulted in a closer bond between us. They have also been kind, generous and supportive as a family. My character has changed a lot over time and I think I have become more kind and loving. I am married now and have a wonderful wife who is also a Christian, as well as a sweet little boy who is four years old.

CONCLUSION

I also developed some close friendships with Christians whom I met from time to time and got involved with a local church fellowship. I changed my name from Khalil to David. I am very sure about my faith in Lord Jesus Christ and I will continue to follow him because I know,

__Truth is Jesus; Jesus is truth;__
__Lord is Jesus; Jesus is Lord.__

Story of Imran

FROM CONTROVERCY TO CONVERSION

INTRODUCTION

My conversion to Christianity started with a wrong phone number. Shakir Hussain, a friend of mine, was calling Imran Shah, another friend of mine. Imran's name was listed right after mine in Shakir's phone book, and he dialed my number by mistake. Shakir, Imran Shah and I were classmates and good friends. Since we graduated, I hadn't talked to them in a long time, so he decided to tell me what was going on in his life and wanted to know about my life as well.

Shakir was graduating as a computer engineer that year and this made me really happy for him. He told me that there is going to be a big change in his life. It shocked me when he said that he was seriously thinking about becoming a Christian. I angrily told him how he could think of converting into a religion that is in vain and corrupted in all means. He told me that he will convince me and Imran Shah to also convert into

Christianity. He started this long story and boring conversation about what made him take this step, but I decided to end this topic, actually ending the phone call at that time. I made an excuse and hung up the phone. Shakir made me really mad!

MY MUSLIM FAMILY

Let me first tell you something about my life, how I was raised and what kind of person I am. My name is Imran Qureshi, born in 1970 in Lahore, Pakistan. I was raised in a typical Muslim family, where we would go to the mosque on Fridays and on special occasions, fast for the month of Ramadan and celebrate the typical festive holidays of Islam. We were a family of four. I had one older sister. My father was an owner of an oil factory where he used to do both wholesale and retail. My mother was a Montessori directress (teacher). We were a fortunate family that never experienced deprivation. As my parents both worked, we even had servants in our house performing all the housework including cooking and cleaning.

My parents were very religious and wanted me and my sister to be the same. I was raised in the traditional way of studying the Quran, praying and doing "good deeds." Helping others was always the priority of our family. I had an uncle who lived just a few blocks from our house; he was not a very religious person. He did not pray or fast. I had often seen my dad and him arguing about religion. This made me really sad. My uncle never got married and the reason was the same—he didn't want his wife to argue with him about religious matters.

Although my mother was a working woman, she devoted all of her time and energy in teaching both of us about Islam. She taught me Urdu and Arabic at the age of five. By the age of six I had read the entire Quran in Arabic and had also memorized some chapters. From that time on, my life as a Muslim was used as a model for all the children in the local Islamic communities.

LOVE FOR ISLAM

Every day when I woke up, I started my day by reciting the prayer that was to be read upon waking up, thanking god for saving me from the death of sleep and for giving me another day to live. I would then proceed to my morning recitation of the Quran following with the first prayer of the day (fajr). Prayers never ended: before eating, after eating, before leaving the house, before reaching the school (in the bus), before starting a lesson and so on.

A devout Muslim's day is filled with the remembrance of god through traditional Islamic methods. I was very happy with what I was doing. I was never lost in complacency and disillusionment with religion. I loved Islam with all my heart. Islam was a very peaceful religion that taught me to worship god and because of that we were a devoted family towards Islam and the happiest family I had ever seen. Islam was not just my religion, but the whole structure of my life. It ran through my blood. I had learned to defend Islam using reasons and evidence. My parents always said never to believe anything blindly, and to focus on reason and evidence as a defense of the faith in Islam.

A BIG DISASTER

In September of 1983, at 2 AM, a big disaster came that ruined our family. A fire started on some area near my father's factory in Lahore. The county fire department was called to put out the fire. But by the time they arrived, this massive fire spread all over and destroyed the whole factory. No one was hurt, but the entire building, which housed valuable equipment, was gutted. It took more than 100 fire fighters and nearly 15 hours to bring the fire under control.

This tragedy was a big misfortune for our family. We all got disheartened and discouraged, but my father told all of us not to loose hope, something will come up soon. My mother was still working until suddenly after six months of this incident she got into a car accident and broke her foot. The doctor told her not to work for at least four months. There was a time when we were the most fortunate and happy family, but now we have nothing. It was very hard to start everything over again.

ARRIVAL IN UNITED STATES

I always thought that Allah is with us and our devoted practice and faith in him will never be in vain, but after this incident I started thinking that we all were wrong. Fortunately, my aunt who was a United States citizen called one day and said that the sponsorship she did for us 15 years ago got approved and we will all be welcomed to the US as permanent residents. My parents became really happy when they heard this news and we all decided to look forward to good opportunities in the United States. I was still upset with what happened and to leave my beloved country, but I moved along with my family we finally arrived in the US in 1984.

LIFE IN THE UNITED STATES

I started school and found two most lovable friends—Imran Shah and Shakir Hussain—who were a great help to me. I started making myself comfortable and began to enjoy life in the United States. My father got a job in a cell phone company and my mom started working in a Montessori school. My faith in Allah started getting stronger again. I was thankful to god for giving us the strength to overcome all these problems and difficulties.

After we graduated from high school, Imran Shah and his family moved to Washington. Shakir Husain got an admission into a university in San Jose and he moved also. I was still in LA and went to school for my bachelor's degree.

A WRONG PHONE NUMBER CHANGED MY LIFE

After this phone call, I got really upset and decided to meet with him and discuss this situation.

I called Shakir and explained to him the horrible mistake he would be committing when he will convert himself to Christianity. Shakir told me that he was coming to LA for a month for his summer vacation to visit me. On one hand I was really excited to see him after a long time, but on the other hand I was also a little nervous about how I would convince him not to make this mistake.

BIG CHALLENGES

After two days, Shakir came to my house and gave me a surprise. It was great to see him. There started our arguments and serious discussions. I thought that it would only take a few discussions and well-placed challenges to prove that Islam is the true, right and direct way to god, but I was wrong by all means. Even though I gave him a few standard objections to Christianity during our discussion, for some reason his answers did not make me feel combative, and his explanations made me feel like listening instead of attacking.

IS THE BIBLE THE CORRUPTED WORD OF GOD?

Our argument started from the book of god, which he said is Bible, but I was very sure about the Quran, the holy book of god and the true way to know god and his qualities. I challenged Shakir that that Bible is the corrupted word of god and no reasonable person could ever trust the Bible. There have been hundreds of books written on the subject of evidence of the divine inspiration of the Bible, and this evidence is many and varied. Thus, the Bible is full of mistakes and is no longer relevant to our modern world.

Shakir started his debate by giving the evidence about how the Bible is accurate. The historical accuracy of the scriptures is likewise in a class by itself, far superior to the written records of Egypt, Assyria and other early nations. An archeologist said:

"No archeological discovery has ever controverted a Biblical reference. Scores of archeological findings have been made which confirm in clear outline or in exact detail historical statements in the Bible. And, by the same token, proper evaluation of Biblical descriptions has often led to amazing discoveries."

Another striking evidence of divine inspiration is found in the fact that many of the principles of modern science were recorded as facts of nature in the Bible a long time ago before scientists actually confirmed them experimentally. For example, the roundness of the earth, law of conservation of mass and energy, hydrologic cycle, number of stars, gravity etc.

It is true that no real mistake has ever been demonstrated in the Bible—in science or history. Although it is a collection of 66 books written by more than 40 different men over a period of 2,000 years, it is just one Book, with perfect and clear unity and consistency throughout. Anyone who studies the Bible diligently will continually find remarkable structural and mathematical patterns throughout its fabric, with an intricacy and symmetry incapable of explanation by collusion.

The Bible is unique in terms of its effect in individual men and on the history of nations. It is appealing both to hearts and minds, loved by at least some in every race or nation to which it has gone, rich or poor, king or commoner, high or low, men of every background.

Thus, the Bible is God's great work in the creation and redemption of all things, through His only Son, the Lord Jesus Christ.

SON OF GOD, THE LORD JESUS CHRIST

I was really shocked when I heard this long discourse delivered by Shakir. I decided to challenge him on a different task. When he said that the Lord Jesus is the only Son of god, I debated that there is only one god who is Allah and he has no family, he is all alone.

There went his claims:

"In the beginning was Jesus, and Jesus was with God, and Jesus was God. Jesus was with God in the beginning." John 1:1, 2

I said that Jesus is just one of God's beloved prophets and the messiah, but he did not listen; he continued on stating that Jesus is the lord and has an outstanding personality. He has given striking evidence of the great powers in the miracles he performs. God did not get married and have a son; instead, Jesus is the son of God in a sense that he was conceived by the Holy Spirit and he is God made manifest in human form according to the Bible.

Then he started talking about the Trinity, that God, Jesus and the Holy Spirit are three in one.

FATHER, SON AND THE HOLY SPIRIT

There are three who were present in the beginning: the Father, Jesus the Son, and the Holy Spirit; and These Three are One God. (1 John 5:7)

The Trinity is a name given to signify the central Doctrine of Christianity. In the cycle of the head of god there are three persons included: the Father, the Son (Jesus), and the Holy Spirit. These three are highly connected to one another. For example: An egg is one, but it has three parts that join together to make one egg. There is the yoke, the white and the shell, but all three composite the one egg. Another example is a mango, which again has three components: the outer layer (the skin), the inner layer (the juicy stuff) and the core. All three components make one mango.

Therefore go and make disciples of all nations, baptizing them in the name of the Father and of the Son and of the Holy Spirit.
(Mathew 28:19)

The Trinity is based on the same explanation that believes in one God and reveals through three different persons, but are all connected together.

CRUCIFIXION

Then we started talking about the death of Jesus Christ. I always believed that Jesus was never crucified or killed by Jews; instead, God raised him according to the Quran.

Shakir totally disagreed with me. He said that Jesus was crucified on a cross.

*And shall deliver him to the Gentiles to
mock, and to scourge, and to crucify [him]: and the
third day he shall rise again.* (Matthew 20:19)

*Then the soldiers, when they had crucified
Jesus, took his garments, and made four parts, to
every soldier a part; and also [his] coat: now the
coat was without seam, woven from the top
throughout.* (John 19:23)

The Quran states that it wasn't Jesus that the
Jews crucified, but someone that resembled him.

*"And because of their saying (in boast), "We
killed Messiah 'Iesa (Jesus), son of Maryam (Mary),
the Messenger of Allah," - but they killed him not,
nor crucified him, but the resemblance of 'Iesa
(Jesus) was put over another man (and they killed
that man), and those who differ therein are full of
doubts. They have no (certain) knowledge, they
follow nothing but conjecture. For surely; they
killed him not [i.e. 'Iesa (Jesus), son of Maryam
(Mary)
But Allah raised him ['Iesa (Jesus)] up (with his
Body and soul) unto Himself (and he is in the
heavens). And Allah is Ever All Powerful, All
Wise.)"* (Q.4:157-158)

However, the Bible clearly teaches that Jesus died
on a cross (Matthew 27:32, 40, 42; Mark 15:21, 30,
32; Luke 23:26; John 19:17, 19, 25). The Greek
words in these Scriptures specifically identifies a
cross, not a pole or stake. The most common
method of execution by the Romans at that time

was crucifying a person on a cross, with nails through their hands and feet. Sometimes people were tied to the cross in addition to being nailed to it. There were times when people were crucified to poles, stakes and trees. But this was not the case with Jesus—he was crucified on a cross by two robbers. He finally died. On the third day after Jesus died an angel descended and he was raised from the dead. Jesus' crucifixion redeems Christians of their sins, which was another new point he raised. I was really sad when I saw a big change in Shakir's thinking.

WHO IS RESPONSIBLE FOR THE SINS OF THE WHOLE WORLD?

But if we walk in the light, as he is in the light, we have fellowship one with another, and the blood of Jesus Christ his Son cleanseth us from all sin. If we say that we have no sin, we deceive ourselves, and the truth is not in us. If we confess our sins, he is faithful and just to forgive us [our] sins, and to cleanse us from all unrighteousness. (1 John 1:7-9)

I was really shocked when Shakir said that according to Bible, God loves the world and its people so much that he gave his one and only son, and whoever will believe in him will not be punished and will have a never ending life.

And from Jesus Christ, [who is] the faithful witness, [and] the first begotten of the dead, and the prince of the kings of the earth. Unto him that loved

us, and washed us from our sins in his own blood…
(Revelation 1:5)

I asked him how only one person could be
responsible for the sins and the bad deeds of the
people of the whole world. I told him that all of
mankind is born pure and everyone is responsible
for his/her own sins.

*Let him know, that he which converteth the
sinner from the error of his way shall save a soul
from death, and shall hide a multitude of sins.*
(James 5:20)

Shakir smiled and said only Christians (who
believe in Jesus Christ) will be saved and cleansed
from all sins, not anybody else, so why don't you
join us, he said. I told him not to joke around with
me, but he said it's not a joke, it's a reality.

*Whoever believes and is baptized will be saved, but
whoever does not believe will be condemned.*
(Mathew16:16)

Should I give up? I asked myself. All those
incidents came in my mind like the factory on fire,
my mother's accident, how I had to leave our
beloved country and friends/family; my faith started
to deteriorate and my heart wanted me to believe
what Shakir was saying.

No, my mind said to itself. I cannot leave
my Islam, the religion of my parents and mine. This
is not right, so I started arguing with Shakir once
again. How can an innocent person suffer so much,

pay for the sins for billions of people and not just one? This cannot be true.

IS JESUS OUR SAVIOR?

Shakir again started his arguments as well as his jokes by saying that as a Christian, life is really easy to live. We don't have to worry about praying at specific times and fasting on specific occasions like Islam. It is simple and easy. You can pray and think about God whenever you want to. You can eat or drink anything you like with no restrictions.

He smiled and said if one plans his life in a good way, helps others and tries to commit good deeds, God directs him and makes his life easier and better. This is the lesson Christianity teaches us.

A man's heart plans his way, but the Lord directs his steps.
(Proverbs 16:9)

I knew that he was trying to convince me in different ways. He kept on repeating:

"Jesus is our savior, Jesus is our savior."

From that day on, I had tons of questions in my mind regarding religious issues. The words of Shakir kept on coming in my mind and crosses came in my eyes again and again. Jesus on the cross, Jesus on the cross; my tongue wanted to repeat these words.

ISLAM OR CHRISTIANITY; WHICH IS THE TRUE RELIGION?

After a few weeks, my other friend Imran Shah called me and said that he had good news for me. He found his true religion and his savior for his lifetime sins. I almost fainted. He told me that Shakir showed him the true way to God through the only path called Christianity, which goes with Jesus the lord. I started feeling scared and didn't know what to do. I was acting weird and everybody at home was wondering what had happened to me.

As I had never hid anything from my mom, I thought I should tell her everything. But I was very scared. I could not pray to Allah and Islam any more; my mind and my heart, actually my whole body was forcing me to believe in Shakir's words and convert to the religion that is true and right. In spite of everything, I kept on praying regularly and doing what I was doing before to show my family that nothing had happened.

I couldn't sleep at night, couldn't concentrate on my studies; I actually couldn't concentrate on anything. My mind kept on asking me that what proof do I have that Islam is the correct and true way to God? I only did what my parents taught me and told me to do.

LORD JESUS: THE TRUE WAY TO GOD

I prayed that if Jesus is the lord, very soon he will show me a sign. On the same night a man on a cross full of blood came in my mind and with a sweet voice he said, "I am your lord, your savior and I really love you." Suddenly I woke up and realized that it was just a dream and went back to sleep. The man again came and said, "It is not a dream, it is reality. I am Jesus Christ, son of the God and the lord." I woke up and my eyes were in tears. I realized that whatever I was doing for the past 23 years of my life was wrong and not worth it. I didn't want to hurt my parents so I decided to secretly go to church and baptize, keeping my belief and new faith a secret.

I was grateful to God for providing me with this great friend who showed me the correct way of life and a path rich in worship. The wrong phone number he dialed changed my life and helped me in knowing the reality and truth.

CHALLENGES AFTER CONVERSION

Some weeks went by; I didn't tell anybody, not even Shakir or Imran Hussain, about my conversion because I was nervous. But after a few weeks I got fed up of reciting the Quran and offering Namaz all the time in front of everybody so I decided to tell my family. I thought I should tell my sister first and prayed to Jesus to help me in this difficult situation and to save my family also by showing them the right path of life. My sister slapped me when I told her. She straight went to my parents and told them about it. My entire family turned against me. I told them that they cannot destroy my soul even if they deny the truth. I explained my faith to them and I did everything I could to convince them, but they did not listen and gave me an ultimatum to either leave the house or become a Muslim again. I decided to leave the house. I went to Washington to Shakir's house and asked him if I could live with him for a few days. He and his family welcomed me and were glad that I chose the right path.

CONCLUSION

My parents really loved me and they couldn't live without me. After a few weeks they called me to come back and promised to no longer make an objection to what I was doing.

They gradually accepted me as a Christian. They are still Muslims, but I am very sure that one day I will convince them to get themselves converted into the true religion.

This is my story of "from controversy to conversion" by IMRAN QURESHI.

Story of Ibrahim

I will sing of the Lord's great love forever; with my mouth I will make your faithfulness known through all generations. I will declare that your love stands firm forever, that you established your faithfulness in heaven itself.
(Psalm 89:1-2)

FIRST STAGE OF LIFE AS A MUSLIM

My name is Ibrahim Farooq. I was born in Iraq in the year 1975. I was born into a conservative Muslim family. From the time we were little, my brother, sister and I would go to the mosque (Islamic Center) with my parents every week. There we learned about God, his prophets, his books, the Day of Judgment and life after death. We also learned verses and prayers from the Quran, the holy book of Muslims.

We lived in the south side where there were very few Christians. I was in love with the Quran throughout my childhood to the extent that I used to eagerly wait for the Quran program on TV.

When I was in middle school, I got very disturbed when I heard my teacher explaining how Islam spread wars and battles led by Mohamed or his successors. I viewed all this as war crimes that encouraged hatred, bad deeds and the loss of lives.

As it was the tradition at that time, I went to study the Quran at a school next to a Mosque that was run by a good teacher, Sheikh Abdullah Nayazi. I studied and learned the Quran by heart within a few years.

As time passed, I finished my middle school and was forced to go far for further Islamic studies. I respected my parents a lot so I did what they told me to do. I was twelve when my father sent me over to a nearby town to study since it had an Islamic center with students from all over Asia. When I started studying there, my teachers were very impressed by my dedication and coached me towards more knowledge. I spent ten years there studying the holy book.

SECOND STAGE OF LIFE AS A MUSLIM

I finished my education and went back to my home around the end of 1997. There I also spent days reading and exploring the Quran, Hadith and Allah's revelations.

Throughout my life, I thought about three personalities who impressed me a lot. These three were Prophet Mohammad, Quaid-e-Azam (founder of Pakistan) and Jesus Christ. My interest in Christ began as a result of my acquaintance with the Quran. I discovered that he was an innocent man.

EXPLORING CHRISTIANITY

In 1998, I decided to explore Christianity. I was driven by a desire to strengthen my faith in Islam and to defend it. Up until that point in my life, I had never been to a Christian church. I had a neighbor, Wilson, who was a Christian. I decided to go to him and get some ideas about exploring Christianity. When I went to him, he said that he couldn't debate or discuss these issues since he was not very religious. He suggested talking to a Christian priest. Before I would go to the priest, I decided to study some of the old manuscripts of Christianity.
I asked my father if he wanted to help me in this project, but he refused and told me not to work on this either. As I really respected my dad's order, I stopped working on this activity for few weeks, but I just couldn't live without working on this.

EXAMINING THE BIBLE

A few weeks later I decided to work on it on my own. First, I decided to inquire into the Bible's kind (what is the style of the Bible) and the credibility of its sources. I wanted to examine archaeological evidence and arguments for and against its historical claims. I also explored the testimony of other ancient texts that illuminate the context of the Scriptures.

I also found that there are many variations of the Bible obtained from more than five thousand Greek manuscripts. There is also a large amount of early manuscript evidence by which we can reconstruct the Bible and be certain about 95 percent of the original content. I also discovered that there are whole copies of the books available from around three centuries after Christ's death and the accuracy is actually closer to 95 percent. There are a lot of fragments of manuscripts that can be dated within a couple of centuries after Christ's death that we have in our possession even now.

MORE RESEARCH ON
THE BIBLE

I still had more questions in my mind so I decided to go to the priest.
The priest debated with me for a long time. He said that the Bible is neither a book dropped out of the heavens, nor it is a creation of man. Rather, it is one that, while coming from God, is written by real people.

ACCURACY OF THE BIBLE

One of the strongest arguments for the accuracy of the Bible is its 100 percent accuracy in predicting the future. According to the priest, Christianity is not a blind faith. It is the only religion that can prove itself, and a main source of that proof is the Bible. Although it is becoming less common, there are still people who tell others that they follow Christianity "because it feels right."

He said that God is the source of the Bible and he inspired real people to write it, yet when we read the Bible the circumstances and character of the writers remain evident. I could not accept this. It looked like the Holy Spirit touched my heart towards the truth. I explained to him that Allah's will is to debate those who are not Muslims; bringing them to Islam is the duty of every Muslim.

The priest stated that Jesus Christ said,

"If you hold to my teaching, you are really my disciples. Then you will know the truth, and the truth will set you free"
(John 8:31-32, NIV).

This sense of freedom in the soul that Jesus mentions is one way to evaluate and praise the truth of the Bible.

When I researched the Bible I was amazed at how the Bible is no doubt a true book of God. Certainly it is a remarkable book, which claims to be

"Given by inspiration of God, and is profitable for doctrine, for reproof, for correction, for instruction in righteousness" (2 Timothy 3:16).

I asked the priest if he knew anybody who had better knowledge of Christianity. He suggested an extremely religious man named David who could help me. When I met David, he told me that I should go to the Church during the service and accompany him there. I was amazed when I saw the peace, dedication and attention of the congregation. I was very impressed by the depth and the spirituality of the prayers, hymns and the study of the Bible.

Most Muslims think that Christians spend their time praying to idols and statues of Jesus and the Apostles, which I call **paganism**.

"Believers, have faith in Allah and His apostle, in the Book He has revealed to His apostle, and in the Scriptures He formerly revealed. He that denies Allah, His angels, His Scriptures, His apostles, and the Last Day, has strayed far from the truth" (Al-Nisa) 136.

ONENESS OF GOD

After the congregation, a date and time was fixed for a meeting between me and David. We met and the discussion proceeded to subjects like the oneness of God and the Trinity. We spent time in arguments with no end in sight.

David said that God is a trinity of persons: the Father, the Son and the Holy Spirit. The Father is not the same as the Son and neither the Son is the same as the Holy Spirit; the Holy Spirit is also not the same as the Father. They are not three gods and not three beings. They are three different persons, yet they are one God. Each has a will, power, can speak and can love. They are demonstrations of personhood. They are in perfect harmony consisting of one substance. If even one of the three were removed or eliminated, there would be no God. God is the father; we can call him **The Head**. He is eternal and immutable, without a beginning or end. Jesus, the Son, is one person with two natures: **Divine and Human**. The Holy Spirit is also divine in nature, is self aware and is the third person of the Trinity.

- *If they were the same, they would not appear separately as they do*　(Matthew 3:16,17).
- *In spite of being different, they are "one"* (John 10:30).

David said that because the word trinity is never found in the Bible, some people wonder about whether this is a biblical doctrine or not, but the absence of a term does not necessarily mean the term is not biblical. In reality, due to the nature of the truth that this term reflects, some people believe it is a poor word and describes exactly what the Bible teaches us about this truth concerning God. But the reality is that the three persons always do things together: The Father gives the order that we can say the word... the Word Jesus makes it, and He does not need any laborers. He does everything with the power of the Holy Spirit. This is the way the cycle works.

TRINITY AND TRIAD

David did not stop; he kept on going on and on. He said that the doctrine of the Trinity has often created confusion among not only people of different religions, but also among Christians. They have mistakenly mixed the Trinity with the Triad. But there is a difference.

The **Trinity** is the teaching that there is only one God in the entire universe, none before and none after him according to Isaiah 44:6, 8, and that God consists of three persons: Father, Son and the Holy Spirit. The Father is not the same as the Son who is not the same as the Father who is not the same as the Holy Spirit. Yet, there are not three gods, but one.

Comparing triad with trinity, a **Triad** is three separate gods. Each person is considered a god. Therefore, in the doctrine of the triad, the Father is a god, the Son is a god, and the Holy Spirit is a god. This is not the doctrine of the Trinity and it is not biblical.

God is faithful, by whom ye were called unto the fellowship of his Son Jesus Christ our Lord (Corinthians 1:9).

JESUS IS THE ONLY WAY TO GOD?

David said that many people acknowledge Jesus Christ as a good man, great teacher, or even a prophet of God. This is true, but it does not define who he truly is. Jesus is the only way to God because Jesus himself said he is the only way to God. It is the claim of Jesus, not our invention. This is one of the examples of verses where Christ said

"I am the way, and the truth, and the life; no one comes to the Father, but through me" (John 14:6).

According to David, the Bible tells us that we are all full of sins and evil acts (Romans 3:10-18). As a result of our sins, we deserve God's anger and judgment. The only punishment for our sins committed against an eternal God is an infinite punishment. That is why we need a Savior!

Every person is separated from God by his/her sins and is in need of forgiveness. Living a good, moral life cannot save a person because good works do not pay for a person's sins. Just as we can only pay a $100 speeding ticket with $100, not by walking 5 miles for the judge or even paying $99, only death can pay the death penalty for the sins. Being religious cannot save a person either because religion does not pay the death penalty.

God came to earth to teach us, correct us, forgive us and die for us! Fortunately, because God is very loving and caring and we have a relationship with him (eternal life), he sent Jesus to die in our place to pay the death penalty we deserve for our sins. Jesus agreed to do this because he loves us, and was the only one able to do this because Jesus Christ is God, the sovereign Lord. He is fully God and our lord.

"For unless you believe that I am He, you will die in your sins" (John 8:24).

Therefore, we can receive forgiveness and eternal life only through Jesus because only he has taken away our sins and bridged the bond between us and God. He died to pay for our sins.

If there had been any other way, Jesus would not have died
(Gal 2:21).

Considering the sacrifice Jesus made, we should not think it is not fair that there is only one way, but we should be glad that overall there is *a* way. Jesus Christ came to earth and died in our place. Jesus' death was infinite and the only payment for our sins. Jesus paid the price so that we would not have to. His resurrection from the dead proved that his death was sufficient to pay the penalty for our sins. That is why Jesus is the one and only Savior.

We love him, because he first loved us. (John 4:19)

I got very confused and could not think about an argument to make David stop. I saw a model for what a Christian man living a Christian life is like! I was very impressed by his faith, his joy, his peace and the light that was shining out of him. He was totally different than any one around him.

I told David that Christianity is a very exclusive and restrictive religion. David had answers to my every question and claim that I didn't know what to say. He said that I must understand that Christianity is not the only religion that makes exclusive claims. Religions like Judaism and Islam also make exclusive claims. All religions cannot be true because they disagree with each other on major issues.

CRUCIFIXION OF THE
JESUS CHRIST

I told David that Christians believe in
crucifixion, which is silly and is in vain. David
asked me how I knew that it is not the truth.
Because I was a Muslim I believed that Jesus was
not crucified like all other Muslims believe, but he
asked me if I had any proof that it is not the truth? I
said that the Jews did not kill Jesus, but Allah raised
him up (rafa'ahu...in Arabic) to Himself. I
responded that if you say that Jesus did not die the
usual human death, but still lives in the body in
heaven, I can understand this point of view. He did
die, but not when he was supposed to be crucified,
and that is being "raised up" unto Allah, which
means that he was honored by Allah Almighty as
his Messenger. The same word (rafa'a) is used in
association with honor in connection with the
Prophet Muhammad.

Maybe your parents told you this, David
said, but this is not the proof that Jesus was not
crucified. I did not answer him. He stared at me for
a few minutes and then said that according to the
gospel accounts, Jesus went through six different
trials before he was condemned to die on a cross.
Three of the trials were before Gentiles and three
were before the Jews. He was repeatedly put before
people to be tried and everywhere he was under
heavy guard. They knew who Jesus was. Thus, this
excludes the possibility of mistaken identity. Jesus
had been performing many miracles and was quite
well known in the area. Since the Roman soldiers
had him during the trials, finally on the way to the

cross they crucified him. He really did die on a
cross.

- *"Therefore the soldiers did these things. But
  there were standing by the cross of Jesus
  His mother, and His mother's sister, Mary
  the wife of Clopas, and Mary Magdalene"*
  (John 19:25).
- *"And as they were coming out, they found a
  man of Cyrene named Simon, whom they
  pressed into service to bear His cross"*
  (Matt. 27:32).

David said that we also know about the
place where Jesus was crucified. We find the
answer in the Scripture. The information is recorded
in these gospels.

*"And they bring him unto the place
Golgotha, which is, being interpreted, the place of a
skull"*
(Mark 15:22).

*"And he bearing his cross went forth into a
place called the place of a skull, which is called in
the Hebrew Golgotha"*
(John 19:17).

The Greek word "**Golgotha**" used in these
gospels means *"place of a skull."* The Hebrew and
the Greek word were the same; therefore, it was a
commonly known name.

I wanted to go home and relax for a little bit, but David didn't stop his claims; he kept going on and on.

Christians do not say that Christianity is the only way because they are narrow-minded, judgmental and stupid, he said, but they say so because they believe in Jesus who claimed to be God (John 8:58), who forgave sins (Mark 2:5) and who rose from the dead (Luke 24:24-29). Jesus said that he was the only way. Jesus is unique. He was either telling the truth or telling a lie. But since everyone in this world, whether a Christian or non Christian, agrees and believes that Jesus was a good man, He cannot be both good and crazy, or both good and a liar. He had to be telling the truth.

He kept on repeating these words

CHRISTIANITY IS THE TRUE WAY TO GOD AND LORD JESUS IS THE ONLY WAY TO GOD.

After this discussion I felt the superiority of Christianity over Islam, but I did not tell David that I was loosing my faith. He told me that we all seek God and told me that in my prayer I should seek the truth. I felt very offended so I asked him if he thought I doubted my faith. I told him that I prayed five times a day to Allah because I seek him and believe in him and his Islam.

EXPLORING THE TRUTH

When I went home, the Holy Spirit moved with me and I started thinking about David's advice. I thought about giving it a try. I spent days and nights with grief and suffering to explore the truth and was never sure if I was even getting closer. I started visiting the Church more often and tried to spend all my time reading the Bible and alternating between right and wrong.

A few weeks later, I met another Christian gentleman who moved to our neighborhood. He was again truly a great person and he reminded me of David. I was again very impressed by his faith. Soon we became good friends. One day he invited me over for Christmas dinner at his house; I noticed that his family was just like him. I asked him about what made him a great human being. He shared his testimony with me and said that he was a born-again Christian. He accepted Christ as his personal Lord and Savior and so he became who he was without any efforts on his part.

This is my commandment, That ye love one another, as I have loved you. Greater love hath no man than this, that a man lay down his life for his friends (John 15:12-13 KJV).

After this dinner, I felt very scared. I prayed to Allah to show me the truth. I would lock myself in my room day and night. I started looking so disoriented and pale that my family and friends were worried and thought that I may have a mental disorder or disease. I had a best friend Nadeem, whom I shared everything about my life. My parents decided to call him. I got very happy when I saw him and told him everything. He explained to me that there is nothing to worry about. If I was searching for the true religion, there is nothing wrong in that. I begged him not to disclose what I had told him.

After he left, I felt a little relaxed and started my research again. I studied more and read the Bible again and again.

FOUND THE TRUTH

After a couple of weeks, I came out from my room. I was very happy and confident. I found the truth to the way and the life. I discovered the sinful nature of man and the salvation through Christ the Lord. I found out and was very sure that Jesus is the Way, the Truth and the Life.

Now the big challenge was to convince my family. That was the hard part. I was nervous so I decided to talk to Nadeem about it. He was not a very religious person. According to him every person is from the generation of Adam and is a human being, and all the religions are directly or indirectly a way to God. He told me that if I thought what I was doing was right then I should go to the church and become a Christian.

Finally, I thought that what Nadeem was saying was right so I went to the Church and asked the priest for baptism. When I came home I told everybody what happened from the beginning. The reaction in my house was similar to the loss of a son, both physically and spiritually. My mother started crying and wailing. My brothers and sisters could not believe the loss of such a distinguished Muslim. My father decided to convince me what I was doing was not right, but he failed.

HAPPY TO FIND THE TRUE WAY TO GOD

I told everybody that throughout the time of my investigation, the only thing I experienced was much distress because I believed in a wrong religion for so many years of my life. During the past few months, I was greatly affected by the attitudes and behavior of Christians around me. I realized that the things I felt about Christians from the community that I had grown up in since my childhood were completely wrong. For a long time I did a comparative study between the Quran and the Bible. I saw just how wrong and unjust my ideas were. During my investigation, I found my true Lord and Savior. I received Jesus as my Savior and Lord and I am very happy. I asked everybody's forgiveness because I got baptized without telling them. But if I would have told them, I know that I would not have found my true Savior.

From that day David became my best friend. We go to church together and I am very happy and thankful to God for sending this wonderful person for me. It's been eight years now. My family is still Muslim, but I am very sure that one day I will

convince my parents and try to show them the true
way to God.

Story of Aamir

IS ISLAM THE TRUE WAY TO GOD? NO!

"Ask god what is the true path and he will definitely show you."

> *Ask, and it shall be given you; seek, and ye shall find; knock, and it shall be opened unto you: for every one that asketh receiveth; and he that seeketh findeth; and to him that knocketh it shall be opened* (Matthew 7:7-8).

INTRODUCTION

My name is Aamir Iqbal. This is my story of how I became a Christian and found my lord and savior. I was born in the year 1981 in a Shia Muslim family in Lahore, Pakistan.

SHIAISM

Let me first tell you a little bit about the Shia Islam religion. **Shiaism** is the second largest denomination based on the Islamic faith after Sunni Islam. Shias lead towards the teachings of Muhammad and the religious guidance of his family or his descendents known as Imams. Muhammad's generation through his beloved daughter Fatima (Mohammad had no son) and Cousin Ali, which continues to grandsons of Muhammad, Hazrat Hassan and Imam Husain. Thus, Shias consider Muhammad's descendents (all Imams) as their spiritual leaders and the true source of guidance, and consider the Sunni caliphs as a historic occurrence and not something attached to the faith or religion. According to the Shia ideology, Imam Ali was the first Imam and there were ten Imams after him. Imam Mehdi, the eleventh imam, disappeared and it is the Shia's belief that one day he will come back and appear in front of everybody.

When people praised him to his face, Hazrat Ali said,
"O God, you know me better than I do myself, and I know myself better than they do. O God, make us better then they think we are, and forgive us what they do not know."

MY FAMILY

Our family was respected by the entire society—actually the whole Shia community—for our integrity of life and strict observance of religious rites and ceremonies. My grandfather (my dad's father) was a great person. He died in the year 1991. He was so religious in his life that people always referred to him as **Janab** (it is a name given to the religious and respectable people to honor them). I still remember him and recall sitting on his lap after he returned from evening prayers and heard him reciting the Quran. My grandmother was the same way; she was also very religious and faithful. She died two years ago in 2005 from a heart attack. My dad was not a good Shia Muslim; I had often seen my grandparents fighting with my father about religious issues. But my mother was again very spiritually minded and devoted towards her faith.

My father's younger brother, my Uncle Husain, was the complete opposite of my father. He was a strict Shia Muslim who did nothing but read the Quran and provide Shia commentaries.

The daily routine of our family always began with the morning prayers and the recitations of the Quran like most Muslim families. When I was four years old, my grandparents sent me to an Islamic school to learn the Quran by heart. They made every effort to raise me in the ways of Islam. Such was the atmosphere of the home in which I was brought up.

I was taught that Islam was the final religion and Judaism and Christianity were worthless. Christians are idolized and worship three gods. I was taught that Christians had corrupted the "original" Bible and the death, crucifixion and resurrection of Jesus Christ were wrong and faithless, but there was never any serious attempt to explain the ground of such claims.

MY STUDIES

When I was only six years old, I was sent to the mission school. Not only Islamic studies, but also the teachings of Christianity, Hinduism and Buddhism (world's other three largest religions) were imparted in that school. The missionary, while spreading Islam, should know about all the major religions of the world so that he knows what these people believe and how to convert them into Muslims. This was the purpose of that mission school. The teachings of all the holy books, especially the Bible, were taken seriously. All this helped me to be careful and sensitive in the matters of spirituality and religion. I enjoyed my knowledge profoundly and my experience intensely, particularly the writings of religious writers, traditional Islamic knowledge and historical information about different religions. The death of my grandfather, when I was only ten years old, created a big shock to everybody in my family. As he was the pillar of our family, we all were very sad and distressed to lose him.

IS ISLAM THE TRUE RELIGION?

When I was in fourth standard, I learned the main concept of the Bible and several of its verses . My mind always wanted to say that the Bible is the true book of God, but my heart, in which there was the Quran and only the Quran, stopped me.

When I reached the fifth standard, we were taught the Gospels in the Persian script. By that time I knew the Christian Scriptures very well. At this age I was already fulfilling my duties as a God-fearing Muslim and I had a good knowledge of the Quran and the traditions, as well as Arabic, Persian, and Urdu.

By the age of twelve, I was an expert in the Islamic prayers and fasting. The strict observance of the Islamic requirements made me proud. I hoped that someday I would go to heaven. Not only in religion, but I was also very smart in my secular education and always was the top student of my class.

CONFUSION

After the death of my grandfather, I felt very lonely because he was not only my grandpa, but he was like a friend who helped me in every part of my life. One day when my uncle (my dad's brother) saw that I was very good in Scriptures and recited many verses from the Bible, he decided to take my religious education into his own hands and gave me some books to read. One of the books contained comparisons and differences between the teachings of Islam and Christianity. After reading this particular book, I had a doubt in my mind about Islam. I continued to read different books about various religions.

At the age of thirteen, my father died unexpectedly. I was devastated. I could not understand why it happened. I kept asking Imam Ali why it happened. I needed an explanation, but there was no answer to my prayers. My mother was so sad and depressed because of this incident that she tried to commit suicide. Fortunately, she was saved. I was in such a state of resentment and anger that I wanted to ask Imam Ali why he first took my grandpa and then my dad away from me at the young age of only 39. Slowly and gradually I got better and started my studies again.

When I passed the eighth standard, my uncle sent me thirty miles away from home to a mission high school for higher studies for one year. In this school, I also carried off every Scripture prize annually. The study of different beliefs made me very confused. I started thinking about how Islam can be the true religion. First, I decided to ask my grandmother or uncle about it, but then I got scared. I outwardly continued to follow the practices of Islam; I knew that I only was a nominal Muslim. At that time I was fifteen years old.

Time passed and my mind became more jumbled by these religious studies. I started asking questions about God, His judgment and His truth. I lived in despair and hopelessness because my soul was seeking the truth. Nobody in my family knew that. I decided to find the true religion by doing more research and studies. Meanwhile I was still following the practices of Shiaism.

FURTHER STUDIES

In time, I decided to go to Karachi. I told my family that I had to go there for my studies and they allowed me. I had the good fortune to meet with people in Karachi who were highly respected and were considered people of authority and great learning. One of them was Mohammad Abbas who was the President of a Christian housing society. He was a Shia Muslim but got converted into a Christian. He changed his name to Dave Williams. As soon as we came to know each other, he gladly promised to give me instruction. He felt that my regular course of studies was nearly complete, and advised me to give more attention to the study of logic. He also gave me permission to use his splendid library. Thus, I began my studies under his guidance.

During this time, I met a few more scholars and professors who were experts in logic and philosophy. I entered the Madrasa-i-Zakariyya and began a study of the advanced books on logic and philosophy. Dave treated me as a son and gave me a room next to his own so that I could call him for help any time.

One day during a walk with Dave, I found some Christian preachers speaking to the people. Immediately, the book about the differences between Islam and Christianity came into my mind. I was ready to advance towards the preachers when Dave stopped me and said that it was waste of time to argue with them. These poor fellows neither knew how to carry on a discussion, nor were they familiar with the rules of debate. They were paid to do this work and were fulfilling their duty, so there was absolutely no use in arguing with them. I wanted to ask him why, but I respected him a lot so I turned my way and we went home.

MONTH OF MUHARRAM

The month of Muharram is a holy month for Shias because Imam Husain was killed in that month. Every year, the night before the beginning of the tenth of Muharram, all the men of the community go around the streets beating themselves and shouting "Husain, Husain! Shahid-e-Karbala* Husain!" (Karbala is the place where Imam Husain was killed).

It was the sacred month of Muharram and my mom was insisting that I come back. I decided to go, but Dave stopped me and said that it will be a waste of time for a religion that is in vain. I was shocked when I heard that. I did not know what to do. I did not want to make my mom unhappy so I decided to give an excuse to Dave and went to Lahore.

DAVE'S TESTIMONY

When I came back, while residing at Dave's house, I decided to ask him why he changed his religion. He said that he was busy that day but he would definitely tell me everything the next day. I eagerly waited for the next day. Finally, the next morning Dave came to my room and started his claims. He said that Islam is totally wrong and untrue. I asked him if he could explain why he thought that Christianity was the only true religion. He started his answer with the Bible.

THE BIBLE

As a Muslim I had to believe that the Quran was the uncorrupted word of God transmitted from God (Allah) himself, whereas the Bible is corrupted and wrong. But when I studied the Bible in my mission classes, I always had a doubt in my mind about the Quran. I did not tell Dave about my doubts; instead, I wanted to listen to what he said. Dave said that the Bible is 100 percent the true word of god. It is true by all means and we can find remarkable structural and mathematical patterns throughout the Bible. It is unique in terms of its effect in individual men and on the history of nations. It is appealing to both the hearts and minds of the people of every background.

Thus, the Bible is God's great work that was sent through His only Son, the Lord Jesus Christ.

I knew all that, but I pretended to be unaware of all this so that I could learn more from him. I had already investigated that the new testaments are not at all different from the original manuscript.

DEATH OF JESUS CHRIST

I decided to ask Dave about his belief as a Christian about whether Jesus died on the cross. According to the Quran, Christ did not die on the cross.

Dave said that Jesus was resurrected three days after being crucified on the cross and Good Friday and Easter Sundays are the days when we remember and celebrate this. After investigating the facts surrounding the death of Christ, I was really amazed by how clear it is that Jesus Christ did die on the cross. Based on the historical evidence and knowledge about how Jesus was crucified, there can be no way to deny the death and the crucifixion of Christ.

IS JESUS THE SON OF GOD?

Jesus saith unto him, I am the way, the truth, and the life: no man cometh unto the Father, but by me. If ye had known me, ye should have known my Father also: and from henceforth ye know him, and have seen him (**John 14:6-7**).

After this discovery, I had a question in my mind whether it was true that Jesus is the only son of God. I thought that Jesus was only a prophet like Prophet Mohammed, who also was a prophet of God and guided mankind. Dave said that it is the truth that Jesus is the son of god. In the Old Testament of Isaiah, it said that a child will be born who would be called **"mighty god,"** but this is not the only testament support for the duty of Christ. The most common title for Jesus was "son of man." According to the New Testament, Jesus was worshipped shortly after his birth, during his ministry and after his resurrection from the dead.

"And Jesus, when he was baptized, went up straight way out of the water: and the heavens were open unto him, and he saw the spirit of god descending a like dove, and lighting upon him and a voice from heaven, saying, this is my beloved son, in whom I am well pleased."

WHAT IS TRINITY?

I started believing what Dave said about Jesus Christ, but I never understood the term "TRINITY." Dave said that as a member of the

70

trinity, Jesus is viewed as God himself. The Trinity says that god is both father and son. This does not make them two gods, but are two separate ways in which God experiences his love. The Holy Spirit is also included in trinity, representing the presence of father with the son and with us.

The Trinity is based on the same fact that the belief in one God reveals through three different persons, but all connected.

Explanation of Trinity

1. *The Bible teaches that there is only one God* (Isaiah 43:10)
2. *The Bible teaches that there is one who is called the Father and is identified as being God.* (1 Peter 1:2)
3. *The Bible teaches that there is one who is called Jesus and is identified as being God.* (John 1:1-3&14-18)
4. *The Bible teaches that there is one who is called the Holy Spirit and is identified as being God.* (John 14:16-17)

I also found out from the evidence that the father is the source of the Trinity. This single source is the basis of God's unity. The son results from him and the spirit proceeds from him.

I believed everything that Dave said, but couldn't believe that Jesus pays for the sins, crimes and bad works of everybody in this world who believe in him. How could it be possible that someone else would be able to pay not only for my sins, but for the sins of the entire world? I told Dave that each person is responsible for his or her own actions. Dave said that the focus of Christianity is fundamentally focused on the crucifixion of Jesus Christ, and the forgiveness of sins that is available through accepting that sacrifice. God is in the process of accomplishing much more than merely saving mankind. Before Adam sinned, God determined that Christ would have to be sacrificed for the sins of mankind (I Peter 1:17-21).

God said,

"Behold, the man has become like one of us, to know good and evil. And now, lest he put out his hand and take also of the tree of life, and eat, and live forever"—therefore the LORD *God sent him out of the garden of Eden to till the ground from which he was taken. So He drove out the man; and He placed cherubim at the east of the Garden of Eden, and a flaming sword which turned every way, to guard the way to the tree of life"*
(Genesis 3:22-24).

God knew what would happen if he allowed these human beings to take from the Tree of Life. Because of their corrupt state, they would be eternally miserable. They would become like Satan in a miserable condition because of their sins. Therefore, God expelled Adam and Eve from the

Garden, placing a flaming sword in their path to guard the way back to the Tree of Life.

Two cannot walk together unless they are in agreement, and when Adam sinned he plotted the course for all who would follow after him. It was a course that had not only some good, but also some evil. The Bible explains how far sin separates man from his Creator:

"For the wages of sin is death, but the gift of God is eternal life in Christ Jesus our Lord."

God gives the gift of eternal life to pay the debt of his own sinful life. Most people believe that "eternal life" means "living forever." However, the length of life is only one aspect of eternal life. Satan will live forever, but their quality of life is the farthest thing from desirable! They do not have quality of life because they are in constant disagreement with God. God's gift is eternal life, and in the Bible Jesus defines that gift further

"And this is eternal life, that they may know You, the only true God, and Jesus Christ whom You have sent."

God's gift is a life where a person knows, understands, has experience with the Father and the Son. The gift is a life that not only stretches on forever, but also has a spiritual quality that makes such length of days desirable! That eternal quality and the perfection have its only source in God, and a relationship with that supreme source is only possible when man's sins are atoned for. For this reason, God sent His Son to pay the debt of mankind's sins so that man might know the Father and the Son in an intimate relationship and be able to live life as they live.

With the true acceptance of Jesus Christ that is receiving not only his sacrifice, but also all of his teachings, this gives us the power and authority to become a child of God.

In him we have redemption through his blood, the forgiveness of sins, according to the riches of his grace which he made to abound towards us it all wisdom and prudence… (Ephesians1:7, 8).

I was really amazed when I heard Dave's claims. My mind always thought that there was something wrong in my faith and belief, and Dave proved it.

.

JESUS IS MY TRUE AND ONLY LORD!

Jesus replied, "If anyone loves me, he will obey my teaching. My Father will love him, and we will come to him and make our home with him" (John 14:23).

In 2002, when I was 21, it was the start of my journey of accepting Jesus as my savior and his full payment for my sins. I am grateful to God that I met with Dave Williams, who was a great teacher, and disciplined me and helped me find the true way to God. After I accepted Jesus as my lord, there was a peace, happiness and satisfaction in my heart.

But this was not it—there was more. I had to tell my family about what happened in Karachi. They were eagerly waiting for me in Lahore. I asked Dave if I could go to Lahore to meet my family and give them the good news. I received permission and went home. I was very scared at first, but then Jesus helped me and I told everybody. My mom and my grandma tried to convince me not to make this mistake, but I told them that this is not a mistake, but is the truth.

My family did not accept me at first, but when they realized that I was totally into Christianity and the Lord Jesus being God, within a couple of years they started respecting my belief.

CONCLUSION

I also developed close relationships with Christians whom I met time to time and got involved with a local church fellowship. I am very happy about my faith and my conversion into the true religion.

Story of Naveed

THE ONLY TRUE RELIGION

"I AM THE WAY THE TRUTH AND THE LIFE; NO MAN COMETH THE FATHER BUT BY ME"
Jesus Christ (John 14:6).

I, Naveed Akhter, am very thankful to the lord Jesus for showing me the true way to god through Christianity, which is not a religion, but a relationship.

INTRODUCTION

Before you understand how I searched for the truth, you need to know a few things about my life—where and how I was raised. This is my story of how I came to find true peace. My name is Naveed Akhter, born in the United States in San Francisco in a Pakistani family.

My parents moved to the United States right after they got married in 1972, and three years later I was born. My parents were very Islamic, religious and devoted towards their faith and Allah. My father was a doctor and mother was a housewife. My father opened his private clinic in 1974, right before I was born, and started his own practice as an MD.

A BIG CHALLENGE!

ACCEPTING THE CULTURE AND WAY OF LIFE IN THE UNITED STATES FOR MY PARENTS

We lived in a multiethnic neighborhood, but lived in a way that preserved our culture and religious identity. We tried to shop in Middle Eastern markets, prepared traditional meals and followed the teachings of Islam. Islam was the main religion; in fact, it was the state religion in our country. Our law was subject to the demands and teachings of Islam, which is why for my parents the transition to American life was not easy at all in the beginning, but devotion to family and religion kept them strong. Faith and hope were the cornerstones of our Muslim family in the United States.

MY EARLY DAYS

When I was born, my parents always worried about me and wanted me to become an honest, loyal religious person and not entirely adopt the American way of life. My parents did not send me to preschool or kindergarten, but instead taught me at home. I started learning Arabic and the recitation of the Quran when I was only four years old.

The daily routine of our family always started with morning prayers and the recitation of the Quran. Every step of life had a prayer attached to it. Waking up, eating breakfast, going out of the house, coming in the house and so on. The duties of the day ended with the night prayers. Such was the atmosphere of our house in which I was raised.

DEVOTION TOWARDS RELIGION

When I was five I had read the entire Quran. My father, being a doctor, was a man of wide sympathies and was tolerant of all races and nationalities. Although his friends included Hindus, Christians and Sikhs, he was very devoted to Islam and the Prophet Mohammed.

My parents wanted me to start my schooling after I attained a good knowledge of the Quran and the traditions. I can still remember how delighted I was in the regular prayers. At the age of six I fasted for the first time during the holy month of Ramadan. There are thirty days (roza) to fast from which I fasted for ten days. My parents were very proud of me. When I was seven, my parents decided to seek my admission in a private school near our house. I was in the first grade and very reserved at that time.

DEATH OF MY FATHER

While I was still in the first grade, my father died in a car accident. This incident was very hard for me and my mom. My mom was completely broke, but she had to be strong to take care of me. She wanted me to study very hard and get a very good education so that I could also become a doctor like my father.

After my Dad died, my mom had to find some work in order to support us both. She started looking for a job. As she never worked before, it was very hard for her to find a job that would suit her. She decided to do babysitting.

CHRISTIANITY

As a young student, I had acquired some knowledge about Christianity through Muslim periodicals. Christian teaching was imparted in our school. The teaching of the Bible was taken seriously and it was considered more important then the teachings of secular subjects. As I loved Islam very much and my religion was my life, I was never interested in reading and learning the parts of the Bible, but I had no choice. My mom was also very unhappy when she saw me studying Christianity.

A GREAT FRIEND

From the beginning I was very reserved and had no friends. I always liked to work and study alone. When I reached fifth standard, there was a Christian girl in my class named Katherine who was a great person and wanted to be my friend. She was three months older than me. I accepted the friendship and soon we got very close and became good friends.

Few years passed and our friendship got stronger. Although she was a Christian and I a Muslim, we became close companions due to our common set of morals.

One day I went to Kathy's house for a group study; there I saw her seriously and attentively reading the Bible. I was very shocked because I did not know that she was also so much devoted to her religion. Like my father, I always wanted to be a man without discrimination and accept all religions, races and nationalities so I did not care how religious Kathy was. At that time I was fifteen years old.

Kathy was a great human being. She respected not only me, but also my mom and considered both of us as a part of her family. Kathy always sought my interest in Christianity and the Bible, but I never supported her in that case.

LOVE IN MY LIFE

Until I was about seventeen years of age, my view of the Christian faith was the typical misunderstanding. As time passed, I became more faithful in my religious obligations. Each time I finished my ritual prayers, I would ask God to put me on the right path.

When Kathy and I were almost eighteen and were done with high school, we realized that we loved each other and wanted to spend our whole lives together. I was very happy to be with her on one the one hand, but on the other hand I was scared to marry a non Muslim girl. I did not want my mom to be unhappy, but I was also afraid to lose Kathy. She is very kind and a wonderful person. I told her only if she becomes a Muslim could I marry her. She did not answer me at that time so I thought she agreed and I got very excited.

Kathy and I continued to date on and off for almost a year. Then on New Year's Eve, she asked me to marry her. I was so happy although I knew it wouldn't be an easy life together. We had been raised completely different, we had come from two different areas of the world, our religions were different and even our reactions were different. But I was happy that she was converting into a Muslim. I loved her so much that I couldn't stand to be away from her. I experienced what seemed like physical pain inside when we were apart. She became my whole life. I felt very secure when I was with her and trusted everything she said. I said yes to her proposal of marriage and we decided to plan it exactly six months from that day. I told her that my mom wanted me to become a doctor so I would continue my studies after we got married.

I told my mom about Kathy; she was not very happy at first, but when she heard that Kathy would become a Muslim, she agreed. I told Kathy that as it was our tradition, my mom wanted to meet her parents and bring a marriage proposal for her. Kathy said that we could come to her house the following week.

RELIGION OR LOVE

It was Friday when we went to Kathy's house. I was very happy. Kathy's family was very kind and gracious towards my mom and me. They arranged a wonderful dinner for us. While we were having dinner, my mom talked about our marriage. She said that her religion was very important to her and she was glad that Kathy was converting. At that time there was a silence for few seconds and then Kathy's mom said that she did not think that Kathy was converting. I was shocked when I heard that and I asked Kathy about it. I was blown away when I heard her answer, "NO I WILL REMAIN A CHRISTIAN." I told my mom that we should leave immediately and we did.

We were very sad and disturbed. I decided that I would sacrifice my love for the sake of my religion and my mom. Kathy kept on calling, but I did not answer the phone. My heart was broken.

CANNOT MARRY A NON MUSLIM

A few weeks later Kathy came to my house when I was not there. She told my mom that she was very sorry for that day and she loves me to death, which is why she remained silent that day when I asked her if she will convert and I thought that she agreed. My mom is a very kindhearted person and so she forgave her. She told Kathy that our religion was everything for us and she will not be able to bear if her son marries a non Muslim girl.

Kathy got very upset when she heard that. But her religion was also very important to her and her family wouldn't be too happy if she converted.

Kathy is a very smart girl. She asked my mom if she could come to our house every day and help her in her work. My mom allowed her. She started coming to our house and every day she had the something related to Christianity with her. On the first day she brought a cross for my mom as a gift. My mom did not know about Christianity at all so she asked Kathy about it.

THE CROSS

Kathy said that this is Jesus Christ who is the son of the God and he died on the cross. Jesus is the Messiah whose coming was promised in the Old Testament and that he was resurrected after his crucifixion. Jesus is God incarnate, who came to provide salvation and reconciliation with God.

My mom told her that this was not true. Jesus is considered one of God's most beloved and important prophets and the Messiah. My mom did not want to talk to Kathy on this topic so she changed the discussion.

The next day Kathy brought the Bible with her and started this discussion again. She said to my mom that the attractive elements in Christianity are numerous. They are good enough to convince anyone who seeks the truth. The doctrine of the resurrection is enough for such a person. Love is one of Christianity's sublime principles. The doctrine of resurrection is difficult and complicated if it is discussed with those who have never heard about it before. However, it is quite straightforward, manageable, convincing, clear and fully believable once you read it in the Bible. My mom did not answer her; instead, she showed her this verse of the Quran.

"We killed Messiah, son of Maryam, the Messenger of Allah (God)' - but they killed him not, nor crucified him, but was his resemblance. And those who differ therein are full of doubts, they have no (certain) knowledge, they follow nothing but conjecture. For surely; they killed him not. But Allah raised him up unto Himself. And Allah is All-Powerful, All-Wise"
(Quran 4:157-158).

Kathy did not give up; she had more information than my mom had.

And shall deliver him to the Gentiles to mock, and to scourge, and to crucify [him]: and the third day he shall rise again
(Matthew 20:19).

Wherefore, behold, I send unto you prophets, and wise men, and scribes: and [some] of them ye shall kill and crucify; and [some] of them shall ye scourge in your synagogues, and persecute [them] from city to city.
Matthew 23:34

Pilate saith unto them, what shall I do then with Jesus which is called Christ? [They] all say unto him, let him be crucified. And the governor said, why, what evil hath he done? But they cried out the more, saying, Let him be crucified. When Pilate saw that he could prevail nothing, but [that] rather a tumult was made, he took water, and washed [his] hands before the multitude, saying, I am innocent of the blood of this just person: see ye [to it]. Then answered all the people, and said, His blood [be] on us, and on our children. Then released he Barabbas unto them: and when he had scourged Jesus, he delivered [him] to be crucified
(Matthew 27:22-26).

My mom was amazed at how clear it was that Jesus did die on the cross.

WHY DID JESUS DIE?

My mom started getting interested in knowing more about Christianity so she did not stop Kathy. Kathy said that Jesus took the sins of humanity upon himself when he was arrested, tortured, crucified and resurrected during the holy days. This was laid out by God and this allowed individuals to come to know God by salvation through Jesus Christ and his crucifixion and resurrection.

My mom told Kathy that if she committed a mistake, she will be the one responsible for it, not anybody else. Kathy said that Jesus died because of our sins.

JESUS IS A GIFT OF GOD TO MANKIND

Understanding faith and redemption can only be done by understanding this true story of sacrifice and love that was provided by God and the crucifixion of Jesus, His Son. There is no way to explain the measure of love and honor that comes with this gift that has been provided to all the people. Jesus came as a gift from God to the world. By preaching to people and performing miracles, God's love was shown to mankind. The Son of God became a human and suffered and died for the sins of the world, not for glory and honor, but to give humans the chance to live eternally in his kingdom. The crucifixion of Jesus is a vital part of Christianity.

THE BIBLE

My mom said to Kathy that the Quran was the only true and right book of God, which has all the wordings directly from God through Prophet Mohammed, and there was no corruption or fraud within it. There started Kathy. The Bible is called the Holy Bible, Scriptures, or the Word of God, which divides the book into two parts: the 46 Books of the Old Testament (with some variations), and the 27 Books of the New Testament containing books originally written primarily in Greek. Some versions of the Bible have a separate section for the books not considered canonical by the publisher. There are other versions such as the Roman Catholic and Eastern Orthodox that contain books found in the Greek Septuagint.

The Bible is the only ancient, well-organized and authentic framework in which all the facts of history fit very well. The Bible does not record all of history. In fact, there are huge gaps in the history contained in the Bible. Actually, without the Bible and what it reveals from prehistory and ancient history, which is the history that was written in advance, it is not possible that one can truly understand any history. No worldly source can help us as the Bible does!

One important thing about the Bible is that many of the principles of modern science were recorded as facts of nature in the Bible a long time ago before scientists actually confirmed them experimentally. For example, the roundness of the earth, number of stars and Law of conservation of mass and energy. It is very true that no real mistake has ever been demonstrated in the Bible in science or history. Although it is a collection of many books that are written by more than 35 different people over a period of over hundreds of years, it is just one Book with perfect consistency.

Kathy showed the chapters and verses of the Bible to my mom. Some of them include the following:

And these words, which I command thee this day, shall be in thine heart: And thou shalt teach them diligently unto thy children, and shalt talk of them when thou sittest in thine house, and when thou walkest by the way, and when thou liest down, and when thou risest up. And thou shalt bind them for a sign upon thine hand, and they shall be as frontlets between thine eyes. And thou shalt write them upon the posts of thy house, and on thy gates (Deuteronomy 6:6-9).

Pe. *Thy testimonies [are] wonderful: therefore doth my soul keep them. The entrance of thy words giveth light; it giveth understanding unto the simple* (Psalms 119:129-130).

The word of the Lord that came to Joel the son of Pethuel. Hear this, ye old men, and give ear,

all ye inhabitants of the land. Hath this been in your
days, or even in the days of your fathers? Tell ye
your children of it, and [let] your children [tell]
their children, and their children another
generation
(Joel 1:1-3).

CHRISTIANITY IS THE ONLY TRUE RELIGION

My mom started crying. She did not have
any words. The next day she told me everything. As
I had learned about this and knew all this from
school, I told my mom that this was all true. I had
learned in my school that because Jesus Christ died
on the cross, I could be saved and would not have to
die for my sins. In studying Islam I had not found
the way to know God. In studying the Bible I found
that only Jesus could satisfy my hunger for Him.

My mom started yelling at me about why I
didn't tell her about Christianity before. I said that
as I was always told that Islam is the only way to
God, I thought that every other religion is in vain.
My mom told me that everything she learned from
Kathy about Christianity is absolutely true and
correct.

As I kept challenging God with my prayers,
strange things began to happen. One Sunday, after
my teaching in the mosque on Christianity, a
Muslim lady asked me to explain the Islamic view
of the birth of Christ. I recited that particular Surah
from the Quran. Although I had read these verses
many times, this time when I spoke, for some

reason within my heart a doubt arose for the first time. I was not sure about my answer. I began to intensify my study of the Bible, comparing references to Jesus in the Bible with the ones in the Quran.

CONFUSION

After our inside conversion to Christianity, we began digging in the Bible for clues that could bring Islam and Christianity close to each other. However, we noticed that the differences between them were getting deeper and larger to the point that there was no way these two religions could be from the same source. The Islamic idea that the Bible was falsified by the Jews could no longer convince us. Very soon, my mom and I accumulated several remarks and doubts that confused us. We started thinking that **The Quran Is Not the Word of God** because God, we were told, was unique although no scriptures were found to be consistent with the nature of such a god. Also, the Quran in some places teaches violence and discrimination against each other and to be unfair to each other. It contains clear-cut mistakes about various kinds of facts.

The history of the Quran is reported in the hadith books that show quite a bit of variation in regards to the collection of the Quran and the different versions of the Quran.

CONCLUSION

We found the true religion. We decided to believe in Jesus Christ and follow Him. When we did so, our lives changed in a very good way. We had peace for the first time. We got baptized and became members of the church.

My mom was very thankful to Kathy for showing us the true path. I married Kathy when we were twenty years old in 1995. We have two kids now, Cassandra and Patrick. My mom lives with us too. We are a very happy Christian family.

Story of Surraiya

JESUS MADE ME DO IT!

Give unto the Lord, ye kindreds of the people, give unto the Lord Glory and Strength. Give unto the Lord the glory [due] unto his name: bring an offering, and come before him: worship the Lord in the beauty of holiness
(Chronicles 16:28-29).

I am writing this brief summary of my life and sharing my experience to serve as a testimony of my Christian journey from Bangladesh to the US. I confess that Jesus Christ is the Lord and the savior of my life. I testify that what you are about to read is true and right to the best of my knowledge as God Himself is my witness. My prayer is that God will speak to your heart and use this testimony to bless you in a special way in your life.

I have always questioned the necessity of religion in our lives and the illogical practices in some religions including Islam and Hinduism.

INITIAL STAGE OF MY LIFE

My name is Surraiya Sidique. I was born in a nearby village of Kanpur, Bangladesh, in 1978. I basically grew up in a strict Muslim home. My father was a Pakistani Muslim. My mother is from London and was a Catholic. My father met my mom in London while away from his homeland on a trip. They got married in 1972, and my mother got inspired and she converted from Catholic to Muslim. Very soon my mom became a very faithful and devoted Muslim. We are a family of five. I have one older brother and one younger sister. Our family was a typical Muslim family, where we would go to the mosque every Friday and on special occasions. We tried to fast for the whole holy month of Ramadan and celebrated the holidays of religion with love and dedication. I was raised in the traditional way of studying the Quran and praying.

In the beginning of my life, I believed everything I was taught about Islam and felt our religion was superior to all other religions of the world.

SECOND STAGE OF LIFE AS A MUSLIM

I followed Islam and knew all the good things about it. Whatever laws I found in Islam I gave a good explanation and everyone was amazed, including me. I ignored all those verses that seemed bad to me and thought I couldn't understand them properly. I am a person who loves to do the right thing and. So I tried to know Islam to practice it better. We had a big family with lots of relatives and almost all of them were Muslim Fundamentalists.

I love my parents, especially my Dad—he is a great person. I looked up to him as my hero. Even though I was a female in a Muslim country, he always gave me the type of opportunities that only males received in that culture. I was a very good student and he wanted me to achieve the most I could in my life. I always had some male friends in my school.

DOUBTS ABOUT ISLAM AND ALLAH

As I grew older, some of the teachings of Islam began to bother me, like the dress code of being covered up. I could never figure out why I had to wear long sleeves and cover my whole face even when it was extremely hot. There was ritual prayer, which I didn't like. I hated to say the prayer again and again every day. It felt so strange like a kind of separation from God. I was taught that if one prayed in Arabic, God would hear it even more, but I couldn't speak Arabic so I felt left out. I tried writing out the Arabic prayers in English, but still something was missing. I went to Muslim scholars and tried to find out the truth. I asked people why the prophet married so many wives and why he married his adopted son's wife. These were the questions that never gave me any satisfaction. One of the Muslim scholars started fighting with me and asked me why I was so eager to find out that there was no God or why did the prophet lie. I told him that I actually didn't want to find out there is no God, but his comments confused me and forced me to question whether Allah was really true.

I really believed that all there is in Islam is truth, and I hoped for the Day of Judgment. I thought only God knows who a person really is; I believed humanity is the main identity of human beings and on judgment day God will send us to heaven. I had such a wonderful explanation about hell and heaven, prayers and fasting and everything that was related to the Quran. This was all because I did what my parents told me to do. I wanted to find the beauty of Islam so that I can be a proper human being, treat others right and teach others the right thing according to the laws of God. But I broke my faith.

There were some questions that nobody could answer, not even my dad. One day I asked my dad if I will go to heaven. He did not answer and remained quiet.

MOVED TO UNITED STATES

Time passed and I was not able to find the answers to these questions. I graduated from university in 1998 and started working as a textile designer. When I was twenty-one, we traveled to the US in search of a better life like most people do. We settled in Los Angeles where my parents got good jobs and so did I.

I was surprised with the culture in the United States. It was a lot different. I met many American guys while I was working as a textile designer and I had to talk with them and feel comfortable with them. But that was not too bad.

One day my mom, while working as a dental assistant, met her childhood friend Salma from London. She had settled in the US in 1980 and came to the dentist to get her teeth checked. As my mom was working at that time, they decided to get together one day and have a chat.

MY MOM'S FRIEND SALMA

A few days later, they both met at Salma's house. Salma was a completely new woman. She had been baptized at her church and had been "born again." That my mom did not understand. She asked her, weren't you a Muslim before? She said, yes! But now she was a Christian and her new name was Mary.

SALMA'S NEW FAITH

During this long visit, Salma shared her newfound faith with my mom. She truly was changed. She was very much at ease and had a peace that my mom could not explain. She was very confident and caring. She said that she loved to know God through Jesus Christ. My mom got very upset about this. She told Salma that she grew up as a Catholic, but changed and promised to stay a Muslim until she dies. Salma got very sad when she heard that. She did not know my mom got married to a Muslim. She tried to convince my mom, but she knew that my mom was too hard of a task for her. Although my mom was stubborn, Salma still challenged her.

After coming from Salma's house, my mom began to pray every day, and read the Quran. She started searching for the peace. While she was searching in Islam for God's love and peace, God did not stop her work in her life. She decided to meet Salma and accept the challenge.

WHICH RELIGION IS TRUE, ISLAM OR CHRISTIANITY?

"In his hand is the life of every creature and the breath of all mankind"

(Job: 10).

After a few days my mom went to Salma's house. There started their arguments and discussions. My mom thought that it would only take a few challenges to prove that Islam was true, right and the direct way to god, but she was wrong.

WAS JESUS KILLED OR CRUCIFIED ON THE CROSS?

"And who through the Spirit of holiness was declared with power to be the Son of God by his resurrection from the dead: Jesus Christ our Lord."

Their discussion started from the death of Jesus Christ. We always believed that Jesus was never crucified or killed by the Jews. Actually, God raised him according to the Quran.

Salma disagreed with my mom. She said that Jesus was crucified on a cross.

Then the soldiers, when they had crucified Jesus, took his garments, and made four parts, to every soldier a part; and also [his] coat: now the coat was without seam, woven from the top throughout (John 19:23).

My mom showed her this verse of the Quran,

"But Allah raised him ['Iesa (Jesus)] up (with his Body and soul) unto Himself (and he is in the heavens). And Allah is Ever All Powerful, All Wise."

After looking in the Bible where it clearly teaches that Jesus died on a cross, my mom was amazed that the Quran is not very clear about the death of Jesus, but in Bible everything is very accurate and clear. Although my mom was a Catholic before, she was not very religious at that time. She did not know much about Christianity; she was only Catholic because her parents were.

"The God of our fathers raised Jesus from the dead--whom you had killed by hanging him on a tree."

Jesus was crucified on the cross by two robbers. He finally died. On the third day after Jesus died, an angel descended and he was raised from the dead. Jesus' crucifixion redeems Christians of their sins. Salma said that the Quran is not accurate at all. It is wrong and dishonest.

IS QURAN THE CORRUPTED WORD OF GOD?

But the word [is] very nigh unto thee, in thy mouth, and in thy heart, that thou mayest do it (Deuteronomy 30:14).

Their discussion forwarded towards the book of God, which she said is the Bible, and my mom said it was the Quran. My mom challenged Salma that that Bible is the corrupted word of God. It is full of mistakes and is irrelevant.

Salma started her argument by giving some of the evidence about how the Bible is right and accurate. She said that the Bible is correct in all means. It is appealing to both hearts and minds and is loved by mostly every race or nation. The Bible is God's wonderful work through his Son, Jesus Christ.

THE SON OF GOD, JESUS CHRIST

My mom challenged Salma on a different task. She said that the Lord Jesus is not the Son of god, but instead there is only one god who is Allah and he has no sons or daughters; he is one and alone without any family.

Salma said that God did not get married and have a son, but Jesus is the son of God in a different sense; he was originated from the Holy Spirit and he is made by God in the form of a human. He is a gift from God to mankind according to the Bible. My mom said that Jesus is just one of God's beloved prophets and the messiah. But Salma showed my mom the verses from the Bible.

"For God did not send his Son into the world to condemn the world, but to save the world through him."

My mom got very confused and decided to talk to all of us about it. She said to Salma that she will see her soon. My dad got very angry and said that Salma is a fool who left this great religion and became a Christian. He decided that we would all go to her house along with my mom and see how Salma could be right.

Salma was very happy to see all of us. The same thing was repeated again with more arguments and claims. But my dad was losing. He could not believe that the religion he worshiped for most of his life could be wrong.

TRINITY

Then Salma started talking about the Trinity. She said that God, Jesus and the Holy Spirit are three, but in reality they are one. In the cycle of the trinity, there are three persons included: the Father who is the head, the Son (Jesus) and the Holy Spirit.

"and the Holy Spirit descended on him in bodily form like a dove. And a voice came from heaven: "You are my Son, whom I love; with you I am well pleased."

Therefore go and make disciples of all nations, baptizing them in the name of the Father and of the Son and of the Holy Spirit

(Mathew 28:19).

The Trinity is based on the concept to believe in one God, which is revealed through three different persons, but all are connected together.

Salma said that Jesus died for a reason. God and his Trinity (God, Jesus and spirit) loves us so much that it made Jesus die to pay for the sins of those who believe in him.

"You do not realize that it is better for you that one man dies for the people than that the whole nation perish."

"That everyone who believes in him may have eternal life."

"He was delivered over to death for our sins and was raised to life for our justification."

We all were really shocked when Salma said that God loves us so much that he gave his one and only son, and whoever will believe in him will have a never ending life.

I asked her how just one person can be responsible for the sins of the whole world. I told her that all mankind is born pure and everyone is responsible for his/her own sins.

Whoever believes and is baptized will be saved, but whoever does not believe will be condemned
(Mathew16:16).

I already had doubts in my mind about Islam. My heart wanted me to believe whatever Salma said.

A Philosopher once said,

"If you push a wall slightly with your finger and it falls down, never think that it happened due to just your finger touching it. The wall had already been pushed many times before and was just waiting for your finger to push it before it fell down." This happened to me.

UNBELIEVABLE

"No" my dad said, "We cannot leave our Islam, which is the religion of my forefathers." This is not right, so he started arguing with Salma again. How can an innocent person pay for the sins for billions of people? This cannot be true.

Salma smiled and said that this is true and if a person plans to live in a good way and help others, God directs him and makes his life easier. This is the lesson Christianity teaches us.

God is perfect, whereas men and women are imperfect. As a result, mankind can only create imperfect religions. This means that all man-created religions are imperfect. There is only one religion, Christianity, which is created by God because it is unique and it has features and characteristics given by God.

For example:

In Christianity, salvation is a free gift given by God. In other religions a person achieves salvation only through his/her good works.

The leader of no other religion dies and then returns after death demonstrating the eternal life we all could have and we could be saved.

Christianity is the only religion that emphasizes love, including love for your enemies.

Only Christianity offers assurance of heaven and eternal life.

There is no other religion where God personally suffers with the people.

You can be born Jewish, born Buddhist, born as a Hindu or a Muslim, but it not possible to be born a Christian. Being born into a Christian family does not make you a Christian. You have to make yourself a Christian.

CONCLUSION

From that day, our family got inspired from the religion although we still had lots of questions in our minds. Salma's claims kept on coming in my mind and crosses came in my eyes again and again. Jesus on the cross, Jesus is my savior—my tongue wanted to repeat these words. Soon these questions were answered and the confusion was gone.

A few weeks later in September of 2002, we all went to church and got baptized. Now we are a very happy Christian family.

Lightning Source UK Ltd.
Milton Keynes UK
07 December 2010

164028UK00001B/123/A